MW00625182

REVIEWS

I was delighted to read "Personal Prayer" by Bruce Downes. It sees prayer as a relationship with a God who is loving, walking with us at every moment of life, inviting us to be aware of His presence and activity so that we can bring Him to others. It is a wonderful, down-to-earth witness of the place of prayer in normal family life. I recommend it very strongly because it makes prayer real, relational and much easier. Jesus is Lord of our life. This is what "Personal Prayer" brings out.

+ Denis J. Hart DD - ARCHBISHOP OF MELBOURNE

Reading your book on prayer was like a breath of fresh air. Congratulations for presenting this essential aspect of our Christian life with such wisdom and simplicity. This is a book that should be placed in the book rack at the back of every church and presented as an essential text in high school religious education programmes. It is obviously a book born of years of experience in both the teaching and practice of prayer. It is a personal witness of your own relationship with God in the context of normal family life. I suggest that when your book is published you send copies for review to every possible Christian periodical or magazine both in the print media and online.

Rev. Des Williamson OCD - Carmelite Priory - Victoria

Sometimes our understanding of prayer can be too narrow and can exclude everyday experiences because they do not fit our definition of what prayer is supposed to be. The beauty of the book, Personal Prayer is that it recognises that prayer can actually be any activity that nurtures our relationship with God and can be either comfortable or challenging, easy or difficult. Through the narration of his own personal experiences, Bruce emphasises that although our relationship with God will go through many different stages, God does not ever turn away.

At a time when so many young people are grappling to understand the true meaning of prayer, Personal Prayer is an invaluable resource for teachers and students of all ages. I wholeheartedly support Bruce in his work which treats prayer as more than a one-way conversation and which recognises God's ongoing presence in our daily lives.

Dr Tony Curry - Principal - Mercy Catholic College

'Personal Prayer' sounds daunting to many people, but here it is presented in easy steps, clear images, and sound method. Most importantly, this book explains the vital link between personal relationship with God and personal prayer, and you can't have one without the other. The intimacy of this relationship is unique for every person, but the way we nourish it - the structure of the relationship, if you like - is common to us all: it begins with personal encounter, and is built day by day simply through spending time with the One who loves you, sharing your deepest hopes and joys and fears with the One who brings us peace. Prayer both creates and nourishes that intimacy, and so is an essential source of life for the Christian. 'Personal Prayer' not only tells us what prayer is, it also teaches the discipline of prayer in a simple, direct and practical way.

Rev Dr Joseph Parkinson STL PhD
Director - L J Goody Bioethics Centre

In this call to contemplative prayer, Bruce Downes plunges us into a journey of spiritual discovery. 'Personal Prayer' calls into relationship with God, into complete reliance on His grace, into journeys that will never cease. That is what prayer is about. Too often we live on the circumference of our lives, rather than at the centre. Bruce Downes shows us how to move into that spacious realm where God has a chance to meet us. Leading us beyond the techniques of prayer to a place where we can receive the gift of contemplation, Bruce Downes offers us simple steps that reflect the wisdom and experience of a mentor who understands the challenges of building, maintaining and deepening a relationship with God. Readers will find within the pages of 'Personal Prayer' insights that speak to their lives. This is a book that will resonate with young people and with adults, with parents, teachers and Religious. It is a book that calls us to that contemplative space which, in a world driven by materialism, expediency and busyness, we so hunger for.

Mary Retel - Deputy Director
Catholic Education Office - Western Australia

For me this small book on prayer is a gem for two reasons. Firstly, it puts into contemporary language and culture an eminently readable, simple and yet comprehensive "how to' instruction on personal prayer that will speak to ordinary people. The second is that it motivates us again to engage the most commonly neglected key factor in effective Christian living - personal prayer. Our ability to deepen our relationship with God, to know God's will in our lives, and to be active and effective Christians in our world depends critically on daily or regular communion and conversation with the Source of Life, our loving God. Bruce helps us to refocus or even restart in a simple way that everyone can access. This is a great little resource to change lives, our Church and therefore the world!

Peter Shakhovskoy - Men Alive, Father and Executive

"Personal Prayer" was an awesome book that has totally changed the way that I pray. Because of this book I have grown closer to God and my relationship with Him has strengthened immensely. When I first read this book I concentrated on the second half about the prayer journal. But only concentrating on that didn't work too well for me, and I found myself becoming more distant from God. Then I remembered the beginning of the book about prayer being an individual thing. Thinking about this, I changed my prayer spot and the structure of my prayer time. By making my prayer time have my own style and keeping in mind all the tips from

Bruce's book, I managed to change my attitude towards prayer. Before I read this book my prayer time was in a slump but after this book it has completely changed. I would definitely recommend this book to any young people struggling with prayer or in a slump with prayer or just anyone. I loved this book and it definitely helped me a lot.

Natalie Purcell - Year 10 student

I feel very privileged to have read your book. It was a good reminder to me of the need to be faithful to personal prayer; you can never hear this too many times! There is nothing more precious than an intimate personal relationship with God. Personal prayer is the way to develop this, and in his book Bruce has set out very simply and effectively how each person can develop the habit of personal prayer. Being in the presence of God who is Spirit and Truth cannot but transform us. It is a message that can encourage and inspire Christian people of all ages and stages. Personal Prayer has touched me, reminding me again of the inestimable value of nurturing my relationship with the Creator of the Universe.

Marita Winters - Director - Catholic Enquiry Centre

The call to serve the church and advance the kingdom of God is as challenging as it is rewarding. It is a compelling force within that drives us beyond our own ability and capacity. What is even more confronting for those of us who are bi-vocational that is, who accept the vocation to serve the church and also work in the business world is the battle of time. This is never more present than the constant balance of relationships with family and friends. But most important the relationship with GOD. I have found your teaching on prayer personally very helpful to simply clarify (when often there is confusion) the fundamental elements necessary for a personal relationship with HIM who is the reason for everything. Thank you Bruce for your years of faithfulness to your personal commitment to a relationship with JESUS. It is evident in your excellent book "Personal Prayer". This is a

MUST read for all Catholics. You answer the often asked questions of How do I pray and How can I have a relationship with Jesus. Thank you.

Robert Falzon
Men Alive Ministry - Husband, Father and Business Man

What a wonderful resource - simple, powerful and a genuine no nonsense approach to prayer. I have read hundreds of prayer books over the last twenty years but rarely have they literally forced me to think about my actions and prayer. I had to stop and retreat and reflect on what I was doing in my relationship with God. The book challenged me to focus on listening to God rather than talking to God. Bruce's reflections on his relationship with his wife were powerful reminders that communication is the key to any relationship and what married guys take far too long to learn -- really listening to our spouse! This deeply personal testimony of a faithful Catholic is inspirational and focussed directly on our relationship with God through others. I thoroughly enjoyed Bruce's personal narratives and links with his faith. But most of all I enjoyed the lack of pious, maudlin theology-speak which so often frightens the faithful. This pray-er book goes to the very heart of every simple man and woman. A wonderful primer in the Catholic way of looking at the world.

Richard Milne
Religious Education Coordinator - Gleeson Catholic College

Everyone urges us to pray but we seldom know how to go about this most natural of Christian disciplines. Bruce Downes provides his readers with an authentic and enthusiastic guide to Christian prayer. He has taken the best of the ancient Christian teaching about prayer and expressed it in contemporary language which is both biblically sound and pastorally helpful.

His book presumes absolutely no knowledge of either the Christian Faith or the practice of prayer. He gently but solidly provides readers with stepping stones and essential practical guidance in the art of prayer. Bruce also challenges his readers to avoid any mechanistic or unsound theories about prayer. The text identifies the importance of regular, habitual prayer and acknowledges the place of doubt and sin, the body and one's emotions in the unfolding drama of being a prayerful Christian. The second part of his work helps the novice in prayer explore essential characteristics of authentic prayer. Christians from any Christian Tradition will draw profit and inspiration from Bruce's work, itself the fruit of his own prayerful response to God's ever inviting and life-changing grace.

Rev. Dr. Kevin Long - Rector - St. Thomas More College
Senior Lecturer (History) University of Notre Dame Australia

PERSONAL PRAYER

A Step by Step Practical Approach

BRUCE DOWNES

WINTERS

PERSONAL Prayer
Copyright © 2008 by Bruce Downes

For more information contact
the Catholic Guy
Email: info@TheCatholicGuy.com
Website: www.TheCatholicGuy.com

All rights reserved. Written permission must be secured from the publisher to use or reproduce any part of this book, except for brief quotations in critical reviews or articles.

Unless otherwise noted, Scripture quotations are from the HOLY BIBLE, NEW INTERNATIONAL VERSION 1 Copyright © 1973, 1978, 1984, by International Bible Society. Used by permission of Zondervan Bible Publishing House. All rights reserved.

Rosemary, you have believed when I have not, been strong when I have been weak, had faith when my doubts have overcome me and believed in me when others wavered.
You are the love of my life.

Emma, Melissa, Adrienne, Joel and Cassandra, thank you for being with me on this exciting adventure called life. Thank you for your love and the sacrifices that you have made so often for me. It has never been dull and the future looks even brighter than our incredible past.

Thank you, Mum and Dad, for you put me on the path of faith. The witness of your life and love for your five boys reminds me constantly of God's love for human kind.

To the Impact Church family, thank you for your faithfulness, dedication and hard work. If I had to do it all again I would want to do it with you.

Acknowledgements

I have discovered that you do not write books alone. This book on prayer is borne out of my parents, teachers and spiritual mentors dedication to prayer as they walked with God throughout their life. It took me a long time to "get it," let alone get serious. Thank you for persisting with me.

Writing about God and prayer can be so technical and therefore difficult to understand unless you are reading this sort of material all the time. I have tried in Personal Prayer to take hard concepts that we may have heard about many times and relate them in easy to understand words. The following people helped me in this task.

Kylie Ryan, you are remarkably gifted. How many hours have you stared at these pages as you put it together so that it would be easily readable? Thank you for your perseverance and devotion.

Thank you to Kylie's mum, Margaret Ryan. How many times did you read the book? I did not know you would get conscripted to this task, but I am so pleased that you did.

Thank you also to Emma McGinniss, Adrienne Downes, Sandra Purcell and Sharlene Andrijich, my English tutors who made many suggestions along the way.

Fr Des Williamson, thank you for inviting me to that first meeting in a classroom all those years ago – one invite determined the course of my life.

Contents

PART TWO · THE PRACTICAL SIDE OF PRAYING

Foreword

In his Letter to the Church at the end of the Great Jubilee of 2000, Pope John Paul II stressed that all Catholic communities need to become schools of prayer, "where the encounter with Christ is expressed not just in imploring help but also in thanksgiving, praise, adoration, contemplation, listening and ardent devotion, until the heart truly 'falls in love'" (Novo Millennio Ineunte, 33). This is because at a time when the whole Church is being called to a new kind of mission, only deep prayer can be the womb of that mission.

We speak of the need for a new evangelisation, but at times the phrase can seem like a mantra: say it often enough and – hey presto! – it will happen magically. Yet there is nothing magical about the new evangelisation – at least not in that sense. There will be a new evangelisation only if there is a new listening to the voice of Christ, which is the heart of Christian prayer. Here we have a book written by a man who understands that Christian mission can only be born from prayer, and that is why he sets about teaching a way of prayer, a way of listening to Christ.

It is significant that it comes from the pen of a lay man. One of the new things about the new evangelisation is that leadership is coming in surprising ways from lay people. The Second Vatican Council urged the whole Church to discover the depth and originality of the baptismal vocation. All baptised people are called in some way to be leaders in the Church and to go out into the world as missionaries in the name of Christ; and all the baptised are called to holiness in order that they might be leaders and missionaries. The emergence since the Council of lay apostles like Bruce Downes is surely one of the fruits of the Holy Spirit, and here Bruce seeks to invite others to join him on that path.

Many people want to pray but are not sure how. They want to move beyond the prayers of their childhood to something richer and more mature. They want to listen more deeply to the voice of Christ in a world where all kinds of noise invade the mind and heart and soul. But they need a companion and guide who can show the way. The Catholic Church has vast spiritual treasures to offer, but we are not always good at opening those treasures to people who are on a spiritual search. We are often good at stirring in people a thirst for the supernatural, but not always good at satisfying that thirst, which is why many Catholics think they have to drink from other springs. Yet here is a book which shows that there is no need to look elsewhere; in the Church, there are endless springs of spiritual teaching which can slake our every thirst. In these pages, Bruce Downes shows himself a good companion and a reliable guide to those springs of living water.

This is a very practical book, with none of the lofty abstractions found at times in talk about prayer. Its style is simple but deep, practical yet rooted in a rich theology. It is both contemporary and traditional, speaking the language of today but drawing much from the Church's long journey through history.

The book is clear in its focus on Christ, as any book on Christian prayer must surely be. In his first Encyclical Letter to the Church in 1979, Pope John Paul wrote that Christianity is not really a religion like other religions; in some ways, it is not a religion at all. At its heart, the Pope said Christianity is an experience not a system – an experience of encounter with the Risen Christ. This encounter, as its grows deeper, leads to a growing sense of amazement in the believer – amazement at the magnificent truth of God revealed in the Risen Christ and amazement at the magnificent truth of the human being revealed in Him. In these pages, Bruce Downes shares with the reader his own sense of Christian amazement. He writes from deep within his own experience of encounter with the Risen Christ, and that gives the book a particular authority.

Because of sin, we are like people who have had a stroke: we have to re-learn the most basic skills of human life, the things most natural to the human being. Prayer is the most natural thing of all, created as we are for communion with God. Yet in a fallen world we need to re-learn what is most natural to us; we need to re-learn how to enter communion with God; we need to re-learn how to give and receive love in the act of prayer. Here Bruce Downes shows himself a sound teacher which is not to say that he presents himself as an expert.

The task of learning to pray is never finished, and in the process of learning, none of us – not even the greatest saint – is ever an expert. We all speak as children. Yet as we learn to pray, we learn more and more of what it means to be fully human in a world where we are often bombarded by one-dimensional or deadly understandings of what it means to be human. The Risen Christ alone reveals the full truth of the human being; and as we see and hear more of Him in prayer, we discover more of the truth of who we are in the mind and heart of God. Here then is a book which not only teaches the elements of Christian prayer but which, in doing that, teaches the elements of being fully human. At that point, we understand the purpose of Christian mission and why we now need a new evangelisation which engages the whole Church in every direction and at every depth.

+ Mark Coleridge
Archbishop of Canberra and Goulburn

Introduction

This book is written to show how simple prayer can be. This is not done simplistically, which would mean to tear the heart and soul out of something leaving it a shadow of what it really is, but written to show how achievable prayer really is for all of us.

Prayer is simple, and yet as a person learns to pray, it can take you to different levels of experience and exposes you to the very power and love of God in a very personal way.

I often think if I can pray anyone can.

In prayer, I have asked God to show me what is next in my life. Am I in the place I am meant to be? In prayer, I have cried in those periods of unspeakable sadness that life throws up when the breathlessness of tragedy has left me empty. In prayer, I have sought wisdom when knowing how to deal with circumstances where no easy answer seems obvious.

Prayer has changed my life and it will yours.

There are many ways to pray.

No one way is the right way.

Prayer varies from person to person.

Prayer is our communication with God, who is mystery. We cannot see God yet we can see the things that God does, for example, everything that was and is made. Yes, I know that was a big jump in faith to say an invisible being we call God is responsible for us and all of creation, but that is what Christians believe based on God's revelation through Scripture and Christian tradition, which is another way of saying the experience of the Church – the people of God.
This book is about how we communicate with God in a world that is soaked with all kinds and forms of communication. Television, the Internet, newspapers, poetry, song, drama and film are all types of communication, but how we relate with God is different to these.

Anyone can pray, in any place at any time. Prayer on the one hand does not have to be learnt, and yet on the other hand it does. I have five children, four daughters and a son. All of them are very different. I have learnt over the years how best to relate to them and to talk with them and how to listen to them effectively. As parents know, sometimes it is what your children are not saying that conveys what they are truly saying. Yes, I know it's one of those mystery things again. Over time I learnt how to listen to them and how to express certain things in ways that they could understand me. We have to learn how to communicate with God.

Prayer is personal because it is about you and me in our most total sense. It is about our life, our story, our circumstances, our hopes, our disappointments and hurts and our dreams. Prayer is very personal.

Let me say right at the beginning, I am no prayer expert. What I am is a person who tries to communicate and relate with God. I believe He made me along with all of creation. I believe that even though He cares about 7 billion or so other people and all the stars and planets, birds and animals etc, etc. He cares about me in a personal and particular way. He knows who I am. He knows where I am. He knows the integrity of my heart and the sincerity of my actions. In short, God loves me with the devotion of a perfect mother.

I wish I were a more faithful and devoted person but, as Paul said,

> *¹⁵I do not understand my own behaviour; I do not act as I mean to, but I do things that I hate.¹⁶While I am acting as I do not want to, I still acknowledge the Law as good,¹⁷so it is not myself acting, but the sin which lives in me.*
>
> *Romans 7:15-17 NJB*

Regardless of this, God still loves me, and so I try to be in a personal relationship with Him and communicate with Him because all real and meaningful relationships need communication.

I now call this material Personal Prayer, but in the past when I have spoken in various places about prayer I have called this by its other name, 'How to Spend Time with God Every Day.'

Throughout this book, I will use different terms for God. Language, however, is limited at times in being able to express all that we want to say. The Bible or Scriptures describe God using mostly male terms, but a closer examination of Scripture will show the feminine aspects of God are also included.

Throughout this book, I will refer to both aspects of God. Once again keep in mind, however, that God is far more than our limited language can express.

You would not be reading this book if you were not at least a little interested in knowing how to talk to God and maybe possibly hear from Him. Your enquiry is just the first step. Keep going. The Scriptures tell us that God is interested in sincerity. Just the fact that you are trying pleases God. You might have to just believe me for now but He knows your thoughts and feelings right now. So keep going.

I have been a 'pray-er' for many years, but there have been times when prayer just seems to dry up. It seems to be more of a routine than friendly and meaningful. It seems to be hard work. From time to time sportsmen lose form and start to perform at a level below their ability. In these cases, their coaches always encourage them to stop doing the fancy and flashy things and go back to the basics of their sport. In time their form returns and so do their results. It is OK if prayer is hard for you right now. Just do the basics laid out here.

Personal Prayer is both basic and advanced.

If you were once committed to God in heart and practice but have fallen away, there is a way back to Him who is the source of all life and meaning. It is honest conversation with God – this is prayer. Do not try and start where you left off; rather, start your prayer in a manageable way with a certain amount of time and a regular time for prayer. He will always come to those who seek Him.

> But if from there you seek the LORD your God, you will find Him if you look for Him with all your heart and with all your soul.
>   *Deuteronomy 4:29 NIV*

Finally, I have tried to make this book as practical as I can. It will describe the way that I pray as well as the way that great men and women of prayer taught me. I have used the word "I" many times throughout this book to make it as personal as possible. I feel a little uncomfortable about using the "I" word so much but prayer is intimate. I am not a prayer expert but just a 'pray-er.'

If you do not have a regular way of praying, why not give a regular prayer time a go? All you need is a Bible (if you don't have one there are lots on the Internet), a notebook, which I call a prayer journal, pen and a commitment to a regular time. This book will walk you through the questions you need to ask yourself before you start praying. It will then give you eight easy steps to help you spend time with God each day.

There are many ways to pray. Catholics gather for the sacraments which are times when we can be completely confident of the presence of God in a very real and powerful way.

So give it a go. You might be surprised how straightforward and easy it is to develop the habit of PERSONAL Prayer.

Part I

What is Prayer All About?

CHAPTER ONE

Relationship

I can still remember when Rosemary and I were dating, and in particular, those very first times together. I remember meeting Rosemary at a hall and walking across a room over to her and saying hello.

I remember us going out on our first date – we went to see *Gallipoli*, a film about a famous World War I battle in Turkey where many Australians were killed. Yeah, I know...the film was not very romantic, but the night together was.

To get to know each other, we just spent time together or we talked on the telephone.

There were times when we talked, laughed and argued about all kinds of things. In particular, I recall travelling in the car with Rosemary in those early days of our relationship. Rosemary would ask me what I was thinking about during some of the silences between our moments of conversation. Then we would have this great exchange about what we were thinking.

When I look back, those moments were all part of building a relationship together and are still important today. The only difference is that over time we have come to understand each other better because we have spent time together. We now have a better idea of what the other person is thinking, how we will react to certain circumstances and even how each of us feels without having to talk about it. We now know what the other person is thinking and feeling at times from a look, a glance or just the slump of the shoulders.

The only way meaningful relationships are built is by spending time together. It is what I call, "Time In." Time is the pressure cooker through which relationships grow and develop. Time in relationships requires an investment and a personal decision to be involved. Time in a relationship also requires engaging in those things that have to be done, to achieve the benefits that are possible in a healthy, intimate and meaningful relationship.

Our relationship with God is no different. Just as in a relationship with another person, you come to know God through "Time In." It surprises some people to discover that this is just how our relationship with God grows – by simply spending time together.

Why do many people not experience God speaking to them or experience relationship with God and have not learnt to hear the sound of His unique voice? God's voice is not audible and yet it can be very loud and distinct.

Personal prayer is about how to spend time with God in such a way that you get to know Him. Spending time together builds meaningful relationships. Imagine having strong feelings for another person but never spending time with that person, never talking together, never being together, and never seeing the other person up close and personal. Can you imagine what that would be like.? It wouldn't be a deep relationship. It would be just a relationship at a distance. Sadly, many people have relationships with God like that - they have relationships that are distant.

God wants to be close to you. He desires to be there in the struggles and joys of your life. While we cannot see Him as we get to know Him, through spending time together in prayer, we learn to recognise His prompting voice.

There are no short cuts. You cannot get someone else to do it for you. It is your personal relationship with God and it requires your attention, devotion and time.

CHAPTER TWO

More than the First Date

Prayer introduces us to God. It is where knowledge of God occurs. Prayer is like taking a person out on a date, and through conversation, observation, and feeling or chemistry we get to know the other person. Even that is a limited metaphor in terms of how we get to know God. As we meet God, we change in ways that we cannot explain. We are transformed in our deepest character. Our spirit – that which is beyond physical emotion – even our personality is changed when we come into regular, meaningful contact with God.

Many people make a commitment of their life to God as adults. I was raised in the Church but came to a point where I had to give assent to the faith of my parents and say, 'Yes, I believe in God.' I committed my life to God by agreeing with what had been presented to me. I decided to believe for myself that Jesus died for me and that there was a certain lifestyle that I was called to live. I accepted that God loves me and wants to be in a personal relationship with me. For some people, this commitment is a point in time while for others it is a gradual decision over time.

Sadly, many people stop here.

For a moment, let us return to the example of going on a date with someone. After you've gone on the first date, the aim from there is to get to know each other. It's not just enough to go on the date – the aim is not the date. The aim is knowledge of each other. And so it is with God. It's knowledge of God.

Many people, young and old, reject God because they have not come to realise that it's not just about a meeting, it's not just about a date. It's about embracing, it's about knowing, it's about being in communion together.

CHAPTER THREE

To Whom Do I Pray?

God, the Father, Jesus or the Holy Spirit?

Throughout this text, I have used the term 'God' and not referred to The Father, Jesus or the Holy Spirit individually. I know that this will sound a little strange, but I used to be confused as to who I should pray to.

I know that God is three persons in one and that together they are God and by themselves they are God.

Confused? Well a lot of people far smarter than me have spent a lot of time, thought and talk trying to express this mystery and it is a mystery.

The bottom line is, however, who do I pray to? If we all were to get together many of us would express different images of God. Some see God as an old man, others a disciplinarian, others a loving caring parent. The images go on and on. My image of God dominates how I pray to God. When it comes to praying, the three persons of the Trinity help shape images of the one God that we can pray too. I have learnt to pray to God as Trinity and also to each person of the Trinity.

God, three in one persons, made the world. The Father, the Scriptures tell us, is loving, righteous and just. The Father sent His Son into the world to save humanity from sin and eternal separation from God.

> *For this is how God loved the world: he gave His only Son, so that everyone who believes in Him may not perish but may have eternal life*
> *John 3:16 NJB*

Jesus came also so that the life we live now was complete.

> *I have come so that they may have life and have it to the full.*
> *John 10:10 NJB*

Jesus, who is God, became a human being. He provided for us a way of living life with an eternal perspective. He invited us into a relationship with Him so that we could know Him personally and that through His death and resurrection we would become heirs with Him of heaven in the presence of God.

The Holy Spirit is the third person in the Trinity. The Holy Spirit animates or brings our life to life. The Holy Spirit is the way God works within us. The Holy Spirit has been described as the power of God.

I pray to God as Father, who is wisdom Himself, provider and protector. The Father to me is loving and yet righteous, that is, holy and pure.

Jesus is my friend and personal Lord or general manager (this is a limited analogy but is a little more modern than possibly 'Lord'). It was through committing my life to Jesus that the Father and the Holy Spirit became real to me. Jesus is my brother and saviour, and I would be no one without His action in my life and for my life.

The Holy Spirit is my enabler and power to live the life made for me by the Father and won for me by

Jesus. The Holy Spirit makes me more than I am able to do and be by myself. Because of the Holy Spirit, I am more than I could have ever imagined.

I have learnt from others and from my growing relationship with God to pray to God as Trinity and as each person of the Trinity.

Throughout this book, I refer to God with this understanding.

CHAPTER FOUR

Presence

We call spending time with God "prayer." It is talking to God like we would talk to a very close friend. Prayer, however, is more than just conversation. It is being present *to* God's presence and it is being present *in* God's presence.

Personal relationships are more than just a combination of words. Love relationships are about being together. My wife Rosemary and I have learnt that just being together can be among some of the richest experiences we have. It says, 'I am at home and comfortable with you. I do not have to say anything to be accepted by you. I can be myself.' Often when I am leaving to go out for the day, Rosemary asks me if I'm going to be home that night. My 'yes' means 'I am going to be here, available to you should you need me or want to talk with me.' Being present says something about my commitment to her. It says, 'I choose to be with you.'

Prayer is being available to God. It says, 'While I could choose other things to do with my time, I choose you.'

My son Joel plays basketball. The best way I can show him that I support him in sport is to be present. I cannot tell him much about the technical aspects of the game because I never played it, but my presence expresses my commitment to him.

Just being present to God says, 'I am committed to our relationship.'

When it comes to God, however, being 'present' touches us in a more profound way. At a deeper level, we come to realise that God is the creator of all things. He existed before time and will continue to exist when time itself ceases. (An amazing concept!)

He is Omniscient, which means He knows everything. Yes, I mean everything, even down to our thoughts and emotions. Any secrets that you think you have, He already knows. (Another scary concept.) He knows what you are going to say before you say it.

He is Omnipresent, which means He is over there and over here, in the past and the present and the future all at the same time. So when you have felt God is far away, He has been there all along.

He is Omnipotent, which means He is all-powerful - the greatest force.

What more can I say? God is God.

If we were truthful what really can we say to God? "God, I want a new car?" and God would reply with "I already know it." "God my Dad is ill. Can you heal him?" and to this God would say "No medical problem is too great for me." "God, I am going to be meeting some new people tomorrow will you help with that conversation?" He would hear in reply "I was already going to be there."

God simply just is. (Yet another amazing concept!)

Something happens when we are in God's presence. We are not just flesh and blood but we are Spirit. When we die, our bodies will pass away but our spirit, which was created by God, will live on. When we are in God's presence, something takes place that is deeper than our physical being and mental capacity. Being in the presence of God who is Spirit and Truth cannot but transform us. Our spirit meets with God, who is spirit in ways that our finite minds cannot understand.

Sometimes the greatest prayer and expression of love is just being in the presence of the God of the Universe.

CHAPTER FIVE

The Importance of Words in Prayer

Words do have an important part to play in our personal relationship with God, even though there is nothing that we can say to God that He does not already know.

Our relationship with God is different to a relationship we have with another person in one major way.

People are changed by our words, but God is constant.

When we tell someone that we love them, it is an important statement for both the person who says it and the person who is the recipient of our declaration of love.

For the person who tells someone that they love them, it is a statement of their feelings for the other person. It says, 'I will act in certain ways toward you because I love you.'

For the person who receives the declaration of love, it is also an important statement. It says, 'someone feels a certain way about me, has certain feelings toward me and is prepared to act in a particular manner with me.' When a person tells someone that they love him or her, the hearer is changed. It says that another person is committed to them. If Rosemary had never said to me she loves me, our relationship would not be what it is. Because of her stated love for me, I have chosen certain actions such as marrying her and remaining faithful to her in action, heart and speech. My whole life has been changed by her declaration of love for me.

With God, however, when we tell Him that we love Him, it does not change Him for He is unchangeable. God has always loved us and always will. Our admission of love and desire to be in a personal relationship with God changes us. When we tell God the desires of our heart, make our requests known to Him and express in words our praise, worship and adoration of Him, something happens in us. *We* are changed.

CHAPTER SIX

The Grace of God and Prayer

There are many definitions of grace, but for our purposes, grace is the ability to respond to God and live a life dedicated to Him because of what God has done. God freely gives this ability or capacity to us, and without it we would not be able to respond to Him. Grace enables us to bridge the gap between our limited human capacity and an infinite God. We receive ability or capacity from God to believe in Him and have love for Him. Now this is where faith is required. We might say, 'I have not experienced any help from God to be in a personal relationship with Him.' The truth is that grace is available to you, should you desire to know God personally. Ironically, the only way to see grace at work is through developing a personal relationship with

God. As we spend time with God we come to understand God, what He is like and how He operates. The ability to understand God is because of grace. The longer I have been in relationship with God the more I understand just how much it is God that is reaching out to me.

Faith, together with grace, is a gift you cannot demand but you can expect to receive when you spend time with God every day.

We receive grace by being in His presence, and it is for this reason that spending time with God in personal prayer is vital for our spiritual growth. We acknowledge God as the Almighty, creator and comforter when we express our needs to God using words. We say, 'God, I am aware of who I am and that I need you for happiness and fulfilment. Apart from you, there will always be something missing in my life.' We declare in our requests of God that He is the God of the impossible and Lord of everything and we need Him in our life.

CHAPTER SEVEN

What is Prayer?

Prayer can have all kinds of different expressions. For some people, it is in the form of liturgy that is expressed in rituals and ceremonies. Their conversation with God happens in that context. For others, it can be through expressions that move from praise of God to silence. It is here that we are aware of the awe and wonder of God. For some people prayers from a prayer book express what we would like to say when our own words seem hard to find.

Our words communicate our heart to God.

Prayer is the key to relationship with God. It is conversation, it is listening, it is reflecting, it is meditating on Him. It is waiting for guidance. It is there to be done in times of happiness or sadness. It's there to be done during times of hardship and joy. It's there when we are wanting and it's there when we have enough.

As I said in the introduction, there is no single right way, just different ways to pray.

On each occasion that we pray, our lives are changed. Not sometimes but every time.

As I have just said, prayer is both being in God's presence and prayer is the words and actions we use to express our inner thoughts and convictions to God.

Can we pray even if we find believing what the Church teaches to be difficult?

At youth retreats and youth conferences it is not uncommon for young people to feel that they cannot pray to God. I have learnt that this is completely true of adults as well. People often feel that they don't know the right words to say. Many people don't know what to do or if what they say is OK. For young people who come from Christian schools,

their teachers or priests or pastors are the
professional 'pray-ers'. Many young people in these
situations have felt that they are observers. Many
young people are inexperienced with prayer.

One night I was speaking to a few hundred young
people, and I believe the Holy Spirit wanted to teach
me a lesson. In the session, I felt inspired to divide
the concept of Church from God for people to be
able to pray to God more effectively. Now I know
for many people that this approach is theological
suicide. However, stick with me.

I asked everyone present to recall how they felt
during times they had been at the beach and looked
at the waves rolling in one after the other. I asked if
they had ever been to a party and felt all alone in the
middle of a crowd and sensed that there was
something beyond all of the people gathered at the
party. I asked them to recall being at a funeral and
the sense of something beyond themselves. I asked
them to remember what they had experienced during
a time when they had laid out on the lawn and
looked up at the stars. They all felt a sense of
something beyond themselves.

I then said to them, "Let us say that this sense of 'beyondness' or 'otherness' is God's presence. Now let's think about what the Church is. It is a gathering of people who bring all of their individual ideas and experiences of God together and then create ways of expressing those ideas and experiences in Church Services of various types. People do this together through rituals, using signs, symbols, words, music, etc." I continued to say that sometimes we don't feel comfortable with the corporate collective expression because it does not capture our picture or image of God. The symbols, rituals and forms of worship are not what we are comfortable with and so we feel disconnected from what is done in Church settings. I said to them, "For the next three days, let's not concentrate on the Church but rather focus on what our experience of God is."

Now I know at a theological level that we cannot separate the Church and God. The Church was established by Jesus to communicate God and His plan in the world. The very fact that the youth and young adults were at the event and hearing the Gospel proclaimed was done through the Church.

However, I was not prepared for what was about to happen. When I stepped off the stage, queues of young people came forward to say in essence, "I never thought I could talk to God because I do not agree with the Church on this or that subject and so I have stopped trying to talk with God at all." Confusion with the Church's teaching had stopped them trying to relate with God. Further conversation revealed that they were either misinformed or did not understand the real position of the Church and the Gospel regarding many Christian teachings and were making decisions based on inaccurate and false beliefs.

At a later session of this conference I realised that a communal prayer experience was not the experience that would touch them. Once again, they would have an experience where the prayers were not their own but someone else's.

So the Holy Spirit led us to create an introductory way of praying. I still on many occasions pray this way today.

I asked all of the young people to spread themselves out through the room, find a space by themselves and face straight ahead so that they were not looking at me or being distracted by anyone else. I then asked them to look at the ground or close their eyes to block out distractions and find a place of quiet within themselves.

I then said to them, "I know that there are some of you who have chosen not to believe in God and others of you who have chosen not to speak to God for a long time. I ask you to just go along with me, in what we are about to do."

I asked them to imagine being in the room by themselves and not with the hundreds of other young people present there. "Imagine that you are here by yourself, all alone." I waited and complete silence fell across the room. I continued by saying to them, "Now imagine that you are here by yourself and that Jesus enters into the room. He pauses, looks around, sees you, smiles and then walks up to you and stands in front of you. What would you say to Him?"

An even deeper quiet and stillness filled the room. I let them be quiet for two or three minutes. God's presence was there, and then I broke the stillness by loudly saying, "Stop. Look up here. Everyone, listen to me. You are praying right now. Prayer in its simplest form is talking to God."

Tears filled the eyes of many of the young men and women as they were able to express their deepest thoughts, hurts, fears and hopes to Jesus. We stayed in prayer for a long time.

After a while some of the young people began to finish praying, and when the option was given that they could leave they would not. Afterward many said, "I had no more to say to Jesus, but I just wanted to be there with others while they prayed. There was a presence I cannot explain."

I still remember how aware I was that I had experienced God meeting with these young people.

For the next few days I had the privilege of attending one of the most prayerful events of my entire ministry life.

I have done this on many occasions since and have made one adjustment. After I stop people and inform them that they are praying I often encourage people to write down what they are saying to God. This is a simple introduction to prayer but it is very effective.

If you were to meet some of the thousands of young people who have been through this experience, now years later, and you asked them, "What is prayer?" Their immediate answer is, "Talking to God."

My experience now with adults is exactly the same. People need to be introduced to how to pray.

I have also learnt that it is very important, as the leader, to stay with people as they pray in those beginning times. I am always amazed at the stillness, the quiet sobbing and the depth of this experience for people.

Prayer is spending time with God expressing your heart. Prayer is not just "I"-centred but is about the holiness of God. However, when a person is starting out in prayer, it is OK if you have a lot to say about yourself, where you are in life, your hopes and dreams. Maturity is always to move beyond our self to another, and the ultimate 'other' is God.

Prayer is being honest with God about yourself. You cannot impress God, so don't try. God loves like a devoted mother who sees your imperfections but still loves you unfailingly and unconditionally.

My prayer at times in many ways is no different to a conversation that I might have with a very close friend. Have you ever sat up until 3 o'clock in the morning and had one of those heavy, deep and meaningful conversations and at the end of it you know that you have connected with the other person? Or it's New Year's Eve, and you've gone past midnight and you sit with someone and have a transparent conversation about your dreams and hopes? Or if you are young have you gone to a friend's house for a sleepover and spent time, when it gets quiet, talking openly? Or if you have friends over with young children, when the children finally go to sleep you sit down, and as the house quietens, you get into conversation with friends that is truthful?

There is a fulfilment and richness to this kind of connection with another person. We are made to be with others and to affect and be affected by others.

This is what prayer should be like. Honest, without exaggeration, transparent and from the heart.

When you pray, make a decision to be yourself.

Jesus regularly prayed to His Father in heaven. It was a priority for Him. He said it like He felt it and He thought it.

When someone asked Him how to pray, He used simple words that were jam packed with meaning because He was sincere, transparent and open.

> One of His disciples said, 'Lord, teach us to pray, as John taught His disciples. ²He said to them, 'When you pray, this is what to say: Father, may your name be held holy, your kingdom come;³ give us each day our daily bread, and forgive us our sins,⁴ for we ourselves forgive each one who is in debt to us. And do not put us to the test.'
>
> Luke 11:1-3 NJB

In one translation of the Bible it says, "Give us food for today, and forgive us our sins, just as we have forgiven those who have sinned against us and don't let us yield to temptation but deliver us from evil."

If we really thought about this prayer we would see how ordinary it is and yet it is extraordinary because of the truth contained within it.

CHAPTER EIGHT

Relationship With God Starts with a Decision

The first decision you need to make is a decision to develop your relationship with God. As obvious as it is, this decision is vital. When I made a decision to love Rosemary, this decision led to a certain way of life that would show that I did and would continue to love her.

One of the basic premises of this book is that if we are going to get to know God, then we must make a commitment to a regular time of personal prayer. We don't get to know anyone well if we don't make a commitment to spend time together on a daily basis.

The metaphor, as I have already mentioned, of comparing our relationship with people to our relationship with God is good but it is also limited.

One of the biggest differences is the invisibility of God. When we meet with a human being we can see them and we can meet in a certain place. We might arrange to meet or the other person might arrange the meeting. While it would be exciting, I have never had the telephone ring and found God on the other end saying, "Do you want to spend some time together today?"

If I am going to be in a personal relationship with God, I have to make some decisions as to how I am going to conduct this relationship. How I am going to enter into a personal conversation with God and be in His presence? It doesn't happen without decisions on my part. God, however, is always available. The decision is for me to arrange the meeting with God, keeping in mind that as far as God is concerned, any time or place is suitable for His diary.

LET'S GET PRACTICAL

I have learnt that there are important practical things to do to facilitate my relationship with God.

The following will help you do this and is a way for you to construct your time with God so that many of the important elements of prayer are included and are part of your normal life with God. This will help you grow in your relationship with Him.

CHAPTER NINE

How Do I Get in the Habit?

Spending time in prayer every day can be daunting. So how do I begin and make it a habit?

First, relationships grow through commitment and persistence. Every day commit to spending some time devoted to God. There will be days when you won't want to get up early or even stay up that little bit later, or spend time during your lunch break. I would say to you, if you decide to do it then do it! Commit to it.

Habits form over time. Make talking to God a habit. If you persist long enough, it will become part of your normal routine.

I have learnt that if I want to change a behaviour or establish a new one in my life, then it always starts with the decision we have already talked about. But I am not anyone else; I am me. I have learnt to become a student of myself. What works for me may not work for you. So my decision has to be very personal, "What do I have to do to establish this new habit in my life?"

I used to be a sugar addict. I would pour huge quantities of sugar over many foods that I ate and in most drinks that I had. I loved it. Some time ago I chose to give up having sugar in my coffee for forty days. I had tried before but had always failed by the third or fourth day. I used to be a person that would make a New Year's Eve commitment only to break it before I had gone to bed that night.

I cannot tell you how hard giving up sugar for forty days was going to be for me, but something happened when I put a time period on the decision. When I set myself the goal of forty days, I was able to accomplish the goal. What I found by the end of that time is that it had become a habit.

I now no longer have sugar in my coffee (I actually think it tastes better without it now). Setting a time period on the decision helped me change my sugar addiction. I was going to do it for just forty days. "I can do forty days," I said to myself, and sure enough, I did.

Make a decision saying, "I'm going to pray every day for the next forty days and not miss a day." If it means that you have to stay up until 3.00am in the morning to get in your time of prayer, do it! Once you know that you are serious about it you will get it done earlier in the day. If there is any doubt in your commitment to it you will not do it.

I have observed that I am consistently good with my personal prayer from Monday to Friday, but Saturdays and Sundays are times when I can be very erratic because my life is in a different routine. Therefore, I have had to become aware of this and make certain decisions as to when I will pray on Saturday and Sunday. The demands of your work, family or even hobbies can affect your time with God each day.

When I was younger, I used to live with a group of guys and we would wake in the morning to pray. Daily prayer only comes through discipline. No other way. So you get into the habit by just choosing to do it. If it means getting up earlier, then that is what you need to do. You might decide that, "I'll pray during my lunch time every day," and if you do decide that, then do it.

A decision to pray daily:

1) Teaches us discipline; and

2) Says to God, "My heart is for You."

From time to time I take a trailer load of rubbish to the rubbish dump, which is at the top of a winding high hill a few kilometres from where we live. When the trailer is full and heavy, the car labours as it ascends the long sloping hill until I reach the top. After I have unloaded the rubbish, coming down from the hill is much easier. It feels light and easier to drive.

Prayer can be a little like this. When we come to God in prayer sometimes, we have to work hard to ascend the hill of prayer. We have to work past the feelings of restlessness and busyness. Even though I know prayer can be very good for me I still find that I can resist the discipline of doing it and find all kinds of less important things to do when I should be praying.

Prayer takes effort, but when I have gone to God, He lifts the rubbish from my life. As I leave prayer, I, too, feel lighter and more easily able to embrace the highs and lows of daily life.

The daily habit of prayer allows me to access God in such a manner that my life is affected by His presence.

CHAPTER TEN

Where Do I Pray?

You can pray anywhere. God is everywhere. He is ready to listen and work in your heart, life and spirit in any place. He is not limited by space. Some people pray in their office at work and arrive early to do so, while other people stop at an appropriate place and pray in their cars, for others it is the beach. Some people go to their local church and pray there. There is no one correct place.

Specific Place

When I want to speak with Rosemary or one of my children or a member of my staff at Church about an important matter I do not talk to them just anywhere. I always speak with them in a place where we will be comfortable and able to focus on the topic to be discussed away from distractions.

In the same way if you are to develop a personal relationship with God, it is important to have a place, which in a sense is your personal meeting place.

There are two places where I spend my specific time with God. One is in my lounge room at home and the other is on the other side of my desk in my office. I pray as often as I can in these two places.

My whole family could tell you, Dad's 'prayer chair' is in the lounge room at home. In my office, I pray on the other side of my desk because then I do not fall into work mode. By sitting on the visitor's side of my desk I know that this is my prayer time and not my work time. This is my devoted time to my relationship with God.

Another very important reason for praying in the same place as often as possible is because when I am there I quickly move mentally to a place of connection with God. This has happened from being in this place many times before. It is what you might call the habit of place.

In other words, I associate the place with the right mental attitude to pray. In this place, I am used to dealing with distractions, the feeling of not wanting to pray, of moving from busyness to being focused on God. I was taught this by some of my mentors many years ago. They said that by praying in a consistent place regularly, I would get into the right frame of mind and settle down more quickly. I have found this to be completely true.

My life is like most people's lives – extremely busy; home life, Rosemary's activities, all of the areas and interests that our five children have and then my many work responsibilities. Sometimes I am a person who has a lot on his mind. When I stop to spend time with God, my mind can be so full that I spend all my time just thinking about the things I have to do and I don't spend much time praying. By having a consistent prayer place, I am able to more easily settle my mind and put aside the many responsibilities I have and concentrate on God more effectively.

Comfort

It is also important to be comfortable when you pray so that you can concentrate on your time with God. If you are uncomfortable, you will certainly get distracted easily. I sit in a lounge chair or on one of the two visitor chairs in my office.

Sitting on the ground is not as comfortable for me at my age as it once was, so I sit in a chair. When I want to stand, I can. If I am uncomfortable I cannot give my whole concentration to prayer.

Few Distractions

It is also very important to pray where there are as few distractions as possible. Prayer is mental, and we can become distracted very, very easily. I cannot have my personal prayer time in the same room with a television turned on because before I know it, I will be watching the television.

On the other hand, often we want a completely quiet place to pray but homes are not always quiet. It may not be possible to find a place where we will not hear the television, the sound of music playing or people's voices. However, the less noise the better. If you consistently pray in the same place you will adjust to the noises around you, and in time you will learn to block out many of these noisy distractions.

When I was young I shared a room with my two brothers. Praying in that room was at times difficult, so I would go down to the local Church and pray there. This, however, may not be possible for everyone.

Free to Move in Prayer or Be Still

It is also important to find a place where you are free to move in prayer. You may wish to stand, kneel, talk out loud, sing or open your hands to God. A private place to do this is important. If you are concerned that you might be disturbed, you are less likely to fully enter into your prayer time with these forms of prayer. This is not always possible, but when you are free to move in prayer you can enter more fully into the experience.

The Bible tells us that when we pray we should go into our rooms and close the door and pray in private.

But when you pray, go into your room, close the door and pray to your Father, who is unseen. Then Your Father, who sees what is done in secret, will reward you.

Matthew 6:6

Praying in a set place regularly has a number of extremely important benefits.

Effective prayer is a habit. By praying in the one place, as I have said, I get into the habit of connecting with the sense of prayer in that place. It does not mean that I cannot pray in the car, it does not mean I cannot pray in the shower, it does not mean that I cannot pray in any number of places, but I pray *specifically* in my lounge or office. So that I am immediately in the right frame of mind and settle down quickly.

Once you have commenced the habit of praying in one place, you will not want to change it just for the sake of changing it.

A consistent place to pray also means that more prayer will actually take place. A lot of time can be wasted looking for a place to pray. When you pray in a consistent place you know what to expect. By praying in the same place consistently, I do not have to decide on what new place I will pray in today, I do not have to find a place where I know it is not going to be noisy and I don't have to ask myself, "What distractions will there be?" or "Will other people be around?" or "Will I be comfortable?" I know what to expect when I pray in that same place each time. If I have to consider these questions every time I pray, I will pray a lot less. This is because the above issues all require time to resolve. However, there will be days when your preferred place is not the most suitable place because of an unexpected intrusion of noise or some other distraction. In situations like these, you are wasting time by trying to find somewhere else that is as noise free as your favourite place usually is. My advice is to stay in your favourite place and pray as best as you can even though for today it is not the most optimal place to be.

Another great advantage of praying in the same place is that if you are able to share when and where you are praying with your family and friends they will be more likely to respect that time and leave you alone. This reduces a tremendous number of distractions.

We cannot always pray in our special spots, though. For example, I travel on a frequent basis and so need to pray in hotels and places where I am staying when away from home. If I am staying in a place for a few days, I will find a particular place and then try and pray there each day.

So find a private, regular place. For many people, it's a particular spot in their bedroom on the floor, on a chair or somewhere where they can be comfortable.

I do not recommend that you have your personal prayer time in the shower, when you are driving or when you're lying in bed – you tend to fall asleep. I am not saying you should not pray in these places, but I cannot impress upon you just how important it is to have a regular place for prayer. The Scripture says to pray constantly, but your committed time to the most important relationship in your life needs to be done in a place where you are as focused as possible.

CHAPTER ELEVEN

How Long Should I Pray For?

Rosemary and I regularly go out to spend time together just by ourselves. We have five children and a lot of people around us. We also work in jobs that keep us busy and apart. We have been taught by other people and have found that we must spend a certain amount of time together to ensure our relationship stays fresh and deepens over time. So we talk each day and usually once a week for a few hours, we have time just to ourselves. Sometimes we go out to find that time to ourselves or sometimes we stay home.

We talk about matters concerning the children, how we individually are going, about Church life and most importantly about what we believe God is doing within us individually. We laugh together and at times cry together and share our hurts and disappointments as well as our hopes and dreams. We talk about our disagreements and how we hurt each other and then we work through resolving those matters. We talk a lot about our future.

This is devoting time to each other. We are not doing anything else at this time. Can you imagine going out on a special date with someone and saying "I'm not spending time just with you, but you can tag along with me, I've got all these other things that I'm going to be doing?"

If you want to get to know someone, it's devoted time.

We also must ensure that our time together is also long enough to do the vital things our relationship requires to keep our relationship healthy and growing.

Our relationship with God requires time – daily time.

Many years ago, one of my mentors who taught me about prayer told me that I should pray for 15 minutes a day. I remember thinking, "How easy is that! Only 15 minutes." Well, was I wrong! Fifteen minutes can be a long time for prayer if you are not used to it, but if you relax and settle in your mind that you are going to be in prayer for 15 minutes every day, it will be the best investment that you will ever make.

Make a decision to spend 15 minutes with God every day. Not in the shower or lying down in bed but time where you are fully focused on being with God.

Now some people in their enthusiasm try to clock up two or three hours a day when they're just beginning. Can I suggest that you do not do that? Just make a decision and say, "I'm going to pray for 15 minutes a day."

Fifteen minutes every day is a lot harder than you think, so commit to a small period of time and let it grow every day.

CHAPTER TWELVE

Accountability

If only new habits were formed easily. I wish it was as easy as saying, "From today I am going to be positive," and from that day forward I was. "From today I am going to exercise more," and from that day find that I was hitting the gym and taking energetic walks each morning. Or saying, "From today I am only going to eat healthy," and then have no trouble in the future eating the right foods.

You might be like this, but I am not. It often seems so much easier for other people, but the truth is, I suspect that many – even most – other people are just like me. We have great intentions but...

It takes me an enormous amount of effort to establish a long-term habit. Oh yes, I can be great for a day or even a week and then it's as if the real me comes back and my new habit comes crashing down.

An important secret in establishing a new habit is to share it with someone else and allow them to ask you how you are going with it. We live in a world where it can be very lonely and we can at times feel very lonely in who we are trying to be. Simply put – we need others.

The Weight Watchers Program learnt this many years ago. Sharing our desired new habit gives us not just our own strength but also the strength of others. Additionally, there is a motivation that comes from knowing that someone you have approached for support is going to ask how *you* are going with your personal prayer commitment.

I have come to realise that, while our motivation in life for goodness and achievement has to come from within us, we all need our own personal cheer squad cheering for us.

When I was at school, I was a sprinter and represented our school at different sporting events. I can still remember standing at the starting line and my school started to cheer and call out, "Come on Bruce!" and then sing and chant the various school cheers. I would stand a little taller, breathe a little deeper, stare down the track and imagine myself breaking the tape first, the crowd going wild. It was my moment to shine. I would get down in the blocks and wait for the starter's gun to fire, and for a brief few seconds, I pushed myself hard because my school was cheering for me to be my best.

Now I would like to finish this story by saying I won and the crowd did go wild, but it never happened. Someone else always beat me across the line. But I am sure I ran faster and performed better than I was capable of because I had the support of others.

In the same way, I am absolutely convinced we all need our own personal cheer squad in life for so many things. In relation to your personal prayer life with God, approach someone that you trust to ask you on a regular basis how you are going. The point of this is not to check up on you but rather to remind us of our decision to be in a regular personal relationship with God.

I call this person my GrowPAL.

The goal of a GrowPAL is to be a friend or mentor who helps us grow in our relationship with God. GrowPALs add three important elements to our life;

> ***Power*** – We are stronger with another's help than when we are alone, whether this be physical, practical help or just verbal encouragement and advice.
>
> ***Accountability*** – When I know someone is going to ask me how I am going with the commitments I have made, I know that this always helps my discipline.
>
> ***Love*** – GrowPALs want the best for us. They want us to be the best we can be. They want us to know God richly.

It is important to have regular contact with your GrowPAL. I would suggest at least a conversation once a week. This can occur through a variety of ways:

- ☐ Go for coffee during the week.
- ☐ Telephone conversation.
- ☐ SMS message.

☐ E-mail.

☐ Invite the person over for dinner.

Together, you can decide on the most appropriate way to meet, given your individual circumstances.

What to expect from a GrowPAL

A good GrowPAL will:

☐ Encourage you to grow in your relationship with God.

☐ Pray for you.

☐ Pray with you.

☐ Hold you to account for the decisions you have made.

☐ Express Christian love towards you.

They will ask you the tough questions:

☐ How faithful are you being to your commitment to personal prayer?

☐ What or how do you believe God is leading you in your life since we last spoke because of your personal prayer?

They do not have to have the answers to these questions, but I have found that this type of reflection causes my relationship with God to be practical and real.

Remember, a decision made in secret is a decision easily forgotten. If you do decide to deepen your relationship with God and accept the responsibility for your relationship with God, having a GrowPAL, I have found, is invaluable.

CHAPTER THIRTEEN

What Time in the Day Should I Pray?

The answer to this is easy. Ask yourself the question, "When am I at my best?" If at all possible, pray at that time or as near as possible to that time.

If our relationship with God is so important, then we should give God our best.

Many people would say that the best time to pray is in the morning. It will focus your day.

However, not everyone can. I have friends who are not awake on any day before midday. They would be best advised to pray later in the day.

In order to pray at your chosen time, especially when you are first beginning to pray regularly or beginning over again, it normally means that you have to make some decisions about your lifestyle in order for your prayer time to occur. For example, if you need to leave for work at a certain time in the morning and are going to pray in the morning, then you will need to decide to get out of bed earlier. Accordingly, you might have to decide to go to bed a little earlier also to be able to do this.

Routine is the key to regular prayer. Plan when you pray. While you may not be able to pray on all seven days of the week at the same time, having most of your prayer times the same helps with being faithful to your time with God.

What happens if you can't pray at your chosen time on a given day? Simply pray earlier or later. I am a morning person, but I often have early meetings after a late night. So I simply schedule my time with God later in the day. If I can't make time later I wake up earlier.

Just because you set aside a certain amount of time to talk to God does not mean you should not talk to God at other times as well. Prayer is a conversation.

You can pray at times other than just your chosen time. Many people I know who are morning 'prayers' also pray as they are going to bed at night. You can talk to God throughout your day.

I have found most young people like to pray at night because they like to sleep in the morning. Be mindful, however, that if you do decide to pray at night, really late night prayer is often very ineffective as you are simply too tired.

My older daughters pray at night very effectively, but if I did it I would end up sleeping in prayer.

CHAPTER FOURTEEN

What About Mums and Dads?

Finding a quiet place when you have family (and a busy family at that) can be hard.

As I have mentioned, I have five children – four beautiful daughters and a great son, plus three dogs. Besides being Mum and Dad, we have worked diligently to also be friends with our children. We love spending time together and have encouraged our children to spend time with us.

Now that they are older and have their own times of personal prayer, they understand the need to respect other people's space. If someone is sitting somewhere in our house with a Bible, notebook and pen, everyone knows that they are praying.

Sounds great doesn't it! Peaceful and serene so that people can pray and build their relationship with God without distractions.

But it hardly is ever like that. Our home is more often than not a busy, noisy place, and it always has been.

When the children were young, like all little children, they wanted to be with us even if we were doing such an important thing as praying to the Creator of the universe. They would play for a little while, and when they got bored they would come and find us. They might want to talk, bring a toy that needed fixing, or wait for us to find the next activity to keep them busy. "Daddy, I need to go to the bathroom," was a very common issue. I would never have known prior to having children how many times five children go to the bathroom!

Sadly, many parents give up trying to pray because of all the distractions with young children.

Now that they are older, as I have said, it is only a little better.

Television, music, loud conversation or one of our girls saying, "Has anyone seen my red skirt?" (all of the girls, including Rosemary, share clothes, so when someone is looking for a particular outfit it could be anywhere in the house). All of this is noisy.

Joel and I do not share our clothes! (I just wanted to say that.)

People come and go, visitors drop by and the telephone rings incessantly.

In the midst of all of this, we individually try to find some quiet time to spend with God.

One day I was sitting in my 'prayer chair' in the lounge and I could hear the noise of the television as I was trying to talk with God. Unlike Rosemary, I get distracted easily, so I was just about to stand and ask them to turn the television volume down when I felt a voice in my head say, "Children are my idea."

God has not asked me to live in a monastery but in a house with a family. If the quietest time that I can find in the day means that the children are watching TV in another room and you can hear the television, that's OK. God understands. If the children ask you for a drink, something to eat or are fighting just when you are having your time with God, relax. He understands.

If I had to wait until I found a quiet, undisturbed time in my house to pray I would not spend time with God very often.

I am a married person with children, so when I sit to pray I've got to be mindful that my kids might be playing around me.

I've got to pray in the context of who I am.

Now, it is not beautiful, uninterrupted silent, wonderful prayer – but it is who I am – it is my spirituality because my call in life is to be a Dad.

If you are able to have someone look after the children while you are praying that is great, but it is not always possible. When I was at school many years ago, I remember visiting John and Anna, a young married couple with three daughters. I would often get there after school just before John arrived home from work. When he came home he would say hello to everyone, have a cup of tea and then Anna would say to the girls, "Daddy's going to have his prayer time now." Anna would look after the children while John went and had his time of daily prayer.

CHAPTER FIFTEEN

What Happens If I Miss?

The premise of personal prayer is that it is a relationship that needs to be maintained and deepened during our whole life. Praying to God should be a daily intention not a haphazard event.

Rosemary and I built our relationship by spending time together, but there are days when we simply cannot spend time together. Life is just too busy and full. Our work, the activities of the children and church life can fill our days completely. It does not mean we do not love each other, it simply means life is hectic at times and spending time together just cannot be fitted into our day. We still say hello to each other and if we do not see each other we will talk on the telephone at least a couple of times throughout the day.

I used to be very hesitant talking about missing prayer because once you say it's OK to miss, it's as if permission is given to miss whenever it gets a little hard. When I was taught to pray, I was told, "Pray every day for 15 minutes a day. Do not miss! If it is very late at night and you have not prayed, still pray. If you are going to be busy for the whole day, get up early and pray then. Plan your prayer and work out when it will be done each day."

I did this and prayed for a long time and never missed, and then I heard it was OK to miss from time to time. You can guess what happened, I fell in a heap. I started missing often. It was as if the discipline was gone.

I have come to learn, however, that it is not the record of never missing that counts but the attitude of my heart and the love I have for God that counts the most.

I have come to learn that there are two types of missing out on daily prayer. First, there are those busy periods in life where life is so full and pressured. Second, there are those days when I just say, "No, I am not going to pray," which is just a lack of discipline to pray.

When I miss prayer due to my slackness, I simply ask God to forgive me. In my prayer journal I may write exactly that.

CHAPTER SIXTEEN

Stress Prayer

There is a different way to pray when life is very busy, and I call it Stress Prayer. This should not be the norm, but it is necessary from time to time. If you know that you are not going to pray on a given day due to your life circumstances, then when you wake in the morning say to God,

> *"Lord, I love you and I ask you to be with me through this busy day. Watch over me, keep my family and me safe and may the decisions I make today reflect my commitment to You."*

Then go and get stuck into the day. At the end of the day just as you close your eyes, say,

"Thank you for being with me today. I will spend a longer time with You soon. Speak to me and watch over me and my loved ones as I sleep."

Stress Prayer is a small amount of prayer, and just as you can't live on a diet forever, it sometimes is necessary for a time.

CHAPTER SEVENTEEN

What About Feelings?

Thank God we have feelings.

We are not robots, uncaring, detached or disinterested. Our feelings are essential to experience love, rejection and disappointment. We would all be the poorer were it not for our feelings.

Standing on a beach with the sand between our toes and the wind in our face when we are on holidays provides us with feelings of joy, refreshment and life. Standing beside a coffin about to be lowered into a hole causes us to feel sadness, compassion and empathy for those left here. Just today, I spoke to someone who said they went to a concert last night and it was one of the best days of their life being in the crowd, listening to the music together with friends.

Imagine life without being able to feel.

Feelings enrich our life, but they can also distract us from the good we can achieve and experience in life.

My feelings get the better of me at times. I know I should pray and turn to God in times of victory and celebration, sinfulness and weakness. Yet sometimes I just cannot be bothered.

My feelings get in the way of right decisions.

Over the years there have been times when I have felt very close to God, and prayer has been wonderful. It has been easy to get up early, and the thought of missing does not even enter my head. Then there are other times when the thought of prayer is difficult. There are times when I do not feel like praying.

It is at these times that I need to recognise the difference between feelings and commitments. If I followed my feelings I would not have held true to my commitments to my wife, children or employer over the years because sometimes "I have not felt like it."

People I know who have prayed for many years recognise the need for consistency in prayer and just do it. We live in a world that says, "If you do not want to do something, don't," and so we see societal ills through a lack of commitment.

Maturity is knowing those things in life that we must do and then doing them regardless of whether we feel like it or not. I learnt this from my Dad. He never asked whether something was good for him. He asked what was good for us because he had made a commitment in having us and he did whatever it took to fulfil that commitment. It is why he is one of my heroes.

When we commit our life to Christ we effectively are saying, "Through thick or thin we will follow you, regardless of whether we feel like it or not."

God also uses our feelings to mature us. This maturity happens when we are faithful in prayer. Even when it is hard, we grow.

Sometimes prayer can be very dry and difficult. It is as if no one is listening. If I had not been taught to persist I would have given up because it appeared as if it were a pointless exercise.

"When" not "if" you have times of dryness and you find it hard to even muster the right words, lean even more into the following prayer method. It gives you a framework to keep you on track. Fortunately, we never stay in the desert. We do come out the other side stronger, more mature and in love with God in a manner that we would not have known if we had given up when prayer became a little difficult.

Part II

The Practical Side
of Praying

P.E.R.S.O.N.A.L
PRAYER
STEPS

CHAPTER EIGHTEEN

P.E.R.S.O.N.A.L. Prayer Steps

The PERSONAL method is eight simple steps to help us spend time with God. The following pages will explain how to pray using the letters P.E.R.S.O.N.A.L. as steps that will guide you through your time of prayer. The word P.E.R.S.O.N.A.L. is an acronym. This means that each letter is the first letter of a word that makes up the content of your subject.

Over the years, I have come to a deeper understanding of each step. The more I learn about God and the more I pray, the deeper are the insights that I get into each step. Take your time working through each one and realise that as you get older, wiser and experience more of life, you will understand each step more deeply.

Prayer is not a destination but the experience of a relationship. The longer that I have been married to my wife, the richer our relationship has become. It is exactly the same in our relationship with God. The longer we pray, the deeper our relationship with God grows.

As you become used to praying, the first three steps, while vital, will become very natural.

Enjoy!

CHAPTER NINETEEN

Speak to the Chair

My very first step is about how I approach the chair in which I am about to pray. It can be any type of chair. It could be a chair that you have bought as your 'prayer chair,' a chair you have designated in your home or office as the chair you are going to pray in or it could be a seat on a bus or on a plane.

Many people go out and buy a comfortable chair just for this purpose.

I have two identical chairs in two different spots. Many of the big decisions of my life that have affected me and many other people through The Catholic Guy Ministry have been made in that chair.

I recently heard of a man who prayed in the same chair for many years. At first it was just trying to discover God, and then over time as he grew in his relationship, he spent many hours in that chair. When he died, someone who had heard of the 'chair' and what role it had played in this man's life tried to buy it, but for the family it had become a symbol in the house of God's presence. It had become precious to them.

I normally turn up to prayer with my Bible, prayer journal, a pen and a drink.

As I approach the chair I say this:

"Lord, I have come here today to encounter you, to meet you, to experience you, to know you more deeply.

I have not come here to learn about you but to encounter you and your presence in my life.

Lord, guide and speak to me as you want today."

The recent Popes have all spoken of encountering God in our lives as a person not just a habit or a distant belief.

Then I make some sign of reverence such as the sign of the cross, or I genuflect or bow as sign that my time of dedication to in this way is beginning now.

I then sit and write the current day, the date and the time I am beginning to pray in my Prayer Journal.

I describe how to keep a Prayer Journal in a later chapter.

CHAPTER TWENTY

Perspective

I always start my time of prayer with God by stopping and realising just who I am devoting this time to. It has stopped me in my tracks so often. I am a limited human being, with fears and hopes, unable to do so many things but yet I am amazed that I am alive. I am incapable of understanding life itself, and yet I am about to spend the next 15 minutes with the Creator of everything.

The dictionary meaning of perspective is *a mental view of the relative importance of things.*

This definition led me to ask the question, "What does the word 'relative' mean?" *Having significance in relation to something else; in comparison with; compared with.*

So in relation to prayer, this means perspective *is my importance or significance compared to God.*

My first step in prayer is to realise who I am and who I am spending time with for the next few minutes.

The Scripture tells us, God, the Creator, thought of you and me before time was even created. God knows everything about you (even the number of hairs on your head.)

Recognising who God is and who you are in relation to God helps get the conversation you are about to have with God into the right perspective. God, while being the Creator, made us to love Him and know Him. God's agenda is simply love.

When I am praying, I might spend just a few brief moments on Perspective. I find by starting at this point each day that I quickly begin to focus. My circumstances seem to come into right perspective or view when I realise who I am compared to God.

We have a puppy. He is full of life, energy and is a destructive cyclone. He chews everything. Recently we were trying to work out just how much he has grown in the past few weeks. Someone said that they had a photo, but it did not help because there was nothing in the picture to compare with, to determine his relative size. Then we found another photo of the puppy and a chair. Immediately we were able to see how big he was compared to the chair. In other words, we had perspective.

On most days, all I will say when I commence prayer is "God, You are God and You made the universe. This is me. I am your son." Some days I might expand on this to express how dependant I am on God for life, to express that it is out of His goodness that I am even alive and able to be in relationship with God.

Some days I will read the Psalms, which is a book of songs in the Old Testament of the Bible, that talk of all that God has done for His people or about the grandeur, holiness or glory of God. I regularly call to mind just how limited I am as a human being and that God is unlimited.

"Hey God, You're God. Wow! This is just me." I have learnt now to immediately have a heart that says, "I need to be humble before You." When I recognise who God is and who I am in relation to God, I find that my conversation is more honest and real. He knows everything, and His love for me is undaunted. So recognise who God is and who you are in relationship to Him and it will help you immediately in your conversation with God.

In the United States, the emergency number is 911 for the police, ambulance and fire brigade. If you dial 911, you are connected almost instantly to a dispatcher who is listening to you, ready to direct your call to one of the emergency services. In front of the dispatcher, when you ring, your name and your address immediately appears on the screen in front of them. The reason for this is that if the caller is having a problem expressing what's going on, perhaps a woman's husband has just suffered a heart attack and she's out of control and is hysterically screaming, or a little child calls who cannot give instructions, then the dispatcher can arrange for the right emergency service to be sent immediately.

When our son Joel was about eight or nine years of age, we were in Brisbane, Queensland, Australia visiting Rosemary's parents. Unbeknown to us he suffered from a condition called nocturnal epilepsy where in the middle of the night he would have an epileptic fit when he was asleep. It affects children when they are young, but I am pleased to say that they grow out of it.

Joel had not slept well the night before, and he fell asleep at 9am in the morning, which is really odd for a child his age. He was lying down on the floor of Rosemary's parent's house, and he had a fit. It was the first time that we had ever seen it. Well, as you can imagine, we were just frantic. I remember saying, "I'll call an ambulance." I raced out of the room, up the staircase, and found the phone, pressed 000 (emergency number in Australia) and was screaming down the phone, "We need an ambulance, we need an ambulance!" After the woman had taken our address details and just as the call ended she said, "Sir, calm down." I remember responding, "Yeah, she's right," because I had gotten into a real panic.

There comes a time in our prayer life when we pray 911 or 000 prayers, when the circumstances of our lives are simply desperate.

Sometimes we don't need to use words because God has already heard our cry. He knows our name and He knows our circumstances because our name and our address and even more 'our lives' flash up before Him as soon as we are in need.

That's what prayer does for us. It puts us in the face of God even when we do not have the words to say to God, "I need You."

So perspective is really important in prayer. Think about this – God is the creator of everything and we spend 15 minutes a day spending time with Him. It simply is amazing that God would know us individually.

CHAPTER TWENTY-ONE

Everything

"E" stands for "Everything" When you first come to pray, make your first action to simply just stop and collect your thoughts. You might have just come in from some activity outside, or you might be just getting up in the morning and ready to roar into the day. You might have just come in from work, or you might be in the middle of lunchtime. There might be a whole pile of things on your mind. What I do when I pray "E" is simply this: "God, right now, for the next 15 minutes I give you everything." So, "P" is "God you made everything, and this is just me coming to be with you," and then "E" – "God for the next 15 minutes, I give you everything. I'm fully focused. I'm on the job. I'm going to be your friend. I'm going to try as hard as I can."

"E" says to God, "I am going to be as focused as I can possibly be during this time of personal prayer with you." I find this commitment to be very powerful every time I do it.

There is also another way to look at "everything" besides just what you are going to be doing during that specific time of personal prayer.

Have you stopped and thought what "everything" means? It is all-encompassing.

God is interested in our "everything." He is interested in your every hope, every dream, the level of your happiness, your friends, family and circumstances. God wants to be Lord of every aspect of your life.

"Everything" means surrendering every aspect of our life to God, who has the best plans for us due to His love for us.

God wants to be God of your every hope, sadness, joy and frustration.

This is a time when I regularly re-commit my life to God and say, "I am yours." The older I have become, the more I have come to realise that I am capable of a deeper surrender of my life to God. I feel as though I need God more today than I did when I was younger. What was my surrender to God in the past is less than what I can give to God now.

Pray at this time, "God, be Lord over every aspect of my life. Take me deeper into you." You may choose to name areas of your life that you come to understand that you need to allow God in.

CHAPTER TWENTY-TWO

Real

The "R" stands for "Real." Let your starting point be where you are at the moment. I pray because I'm committed. It seems all significant commitments have temptations to encourage us to opt out of them, but what makes them worthwhile, what gets us the reward in the end, is when we stick to it.

Sometimes I need to say to God, "God, I really don't want to be here right now. I just don't feel like praying." I do not always feel good about prayer. I don't always want to be there. Sometimes I've just got to be honest with God because another word for being "Real" is being honest.

On the other hand, I might be feeling fantastic about being there and if I am, then I include this in my prayer.

Just saying to God, "God, I am sorry I don't feel like it today," is being real and honest.

There have been times where I've started my prayer by saying, "God, I'm here. Everything in me doesn't want to be here. You might be someone I need to know, but I just don't feel like it right now. TV is on...sport is on...going to bed is on...not getting up as early is on...being here is off." It's just honest. The point is, God knows everything, so why hide it? We can bluff Him and say, "Oh God, I'm so happy to be here," and He replies, "Sure, have you forgotten I know everything?" So it's just being REAL and honest. I think God loves honesty.

There are times when Life is just simply difficult. Being REAL is saying, "God, this is how I am going right now in my life." It is very powerful to be honest before God.

When I do "R" I also read through a Psalm. Sometimes they are Psalms that give God praise, and sometimes there are Psalms that say, "Oh God, why are you beating me up so much, you must hate me," and at other times, "God I am struggling with life right now." The person who wrote Psalms wrote what they were feeling.

A word of caution. It is important that you are careful when reading the Bible in your prayer time as you can end up spending your whole time reading and doing very little praying. I will discuss reading the Scriptures at greater length in a future chapter.

Be REAL in prayer.

CHAPTER TWENTY-THREE

Repent

I know that Personal has only one 'R' but I have two 'R' meanings. The second is the word 'repent.' When I was young, I used to think the word 'repent' meant that I had to feel negative about myself because I had failed, but it does not. It means to turn in another direction.

While repenting is very serious, it can also be a point of great joy and relief in our lives. Have you ever restored a damaged relationship? It is like a weight is lifted off us. There is a happiness that goes along with this.

At this point in prayer, I come to God and I talk to God about the areas in my life where I need to go in another direction.

Since the last time I prayed I might have done something that is contrary to what I believe God wants me to do. The Bible would call this sin. I might have to come to God and be real and say, "God, I want to ask your forgiveness for this…, I am sorry," and then from that point forward choose to live differently.

When we repent, we say to God, "I acknowledge that the decisions I have chosen are not the best decisions." We accept that we have made mistakes and that our future needs to change.

We might say that when we REPENT we are being very REAL.

God is perfect and calls us into relationship with Him. I certainly know that I am not perfect. When I repent, I choose to move closer to God in the thoughts and actions in my life. I surrender a deeper part of me to God and say, "God, be more in my life. Help me to live your way and with you."

I am amazed at just how much I feel the weight of my wrongdoing is lifted from me every time I repent.

CHAPTER TWENTY-FOUR

P.E.R.

Now let me shock you. It might take you as little as one or two minutes to do "P, E & R." My prayers aren't pious; they are just normal in my own words. Be yourself. It is how God loves you.

Perspective, Everything, Real and Repent are in one sense the introduction to my prayer time each day, all the while being deeply a part of my prayer.

This time of prayer says, "God, I am here to spend this time with you. This is my life, how I am doing right now in my hopes, dreams, disappointments and weakness. God, I choose you today to the best of my ability."

Hold on to your seat, because prayer is about to get deeper.

CHAPTER TWENTY-FIVE

Salute

The "S" stands for "Salute." The word 'salute' is a verb and it means, "To meet with kind words, clasp of the hand, a kiss." It is here that you speak to God about how good He is. To salute someone means to greet them warmly. Another word for 'salute' is to praise or thank someone for what they've done. We can thank God for all the things He's done for us. You might do this through song, you might do it through Psalms, you might do it by simply saying 'thank you' for all the things He's done for you.

If you were going to honour someone, what are some words that you would use? If you want to tell someone that they are great, you would say that. So you can say to God, "God, you are great!" and use words like this to describe God. For example, Holy, awesome God, wonderful Counsellor, Maker of the world, Amazing, Magnificent, Glorious, Majestic, Powerful, Beautiful, Mighty, Everything, There is none like you, etc.

Other statements of praise and worship can reflect what God means to you individually. For example, "You are My God, I love you, thank you, You are the Lord of my life, You are first in my life, etc."

In times of silence or quiet, I just run through all the things that I can say to God that I love about Him. That's how you salute someone. Very often when we think about prayer, we think purely about asking for our needs and wants, but how many people want to be in a relationship where you're always asked for stuff? That's a one-sided, not-very-fulfilling relationship.

The following are examples from my prayer;

+ Holy God the Heavens Declare Yours Wonders and Glory
+ King of Kings and Lord of Lords
+ Worthy God
+ Sovereign King
+ My Lord and My God

✦ My Lord and My King
✦ My Lord and My Saviour
✦ My Lord and Master
✦ My Protector
✦ My Guide
✦ My Everything
✦ I honour You and adore you
✦ I honour You and bless you
✦ I glorify You and worship you
✦ I adore You
✦ I honour You
✦ The Lover of My Life
✦ The Lover of My Soul
✦ The Alpha and the Omega
✦ The beginning and the end
✦ The first and the very last
✦ The Centre of My Life
✦ Wonder Counsellor
✦ Prince of Peace
✦ Name above all names
✦ Thank You
✦ You alone are God
✦ You who make sense of everything
✦ There is no other God but You
✦ Nothing compares to You
✦ You alone are omniscient
✦ You are alone are all powerful
✦ You alone are Omnipresent
✦ In You alone do I trust
✦ Worthy are you Lord God

✦ You are Holy
✦ You are Precious
✦ The one and only one
✦ There is no other like You
✦ My Constant Companion
✦ The defender of my soul
✦ You who spared nothing for me
✦ God of Wonders
✦ Holy Beyond All
✦ Mighty King
✦ Mighty Lord
✦ Glory and Honour to You
✦ Lord You are pure

When we say all of these words of 'salute' or praise to God, does God need to hear them? Not at all. We do it for ourselves because it puts God into context and further perspective in our lives. In the next few days, sit down with someone and begin to make a list. "What are all the things that I can say to God?" You can come up with pages of the stuff. I once did this at a seminar, and we filled pages with statements that you can say to God. Once you have done this, keep the list and when you get to "S" you can take it out and start reading through it and after a while it becomes a very natural thing to do.

That is my "S" – that is my salute to God. Ultimately if you do that for long enough, over a period of time, you will come to a very still silence as you realise after a while that there's not very much that we can say to God. He is so beyond our thinking. Even imagining just being in His presence is blessing enough.

CHAPTER TWENTY-SIX

Observe

How does God talk to us? He does not write in the sky, send letters in the mail, or speak in an audible voice, but rather talks to us in our head, our hearts and the circumstances of our lives.

"O" stands for "Observe." By the time I get to "O," I'm pretty sure I'm going to be fairly quiet at that point. This is often the most important part of our time with God. This is the time when we listen to God.

Now the problem with the word *listen* is that we tend to think that we are going to hear something with our ears. The reason I like the word "observe" far more than *listen* is that God speaks to me far more subtly and so the word "observe" allows me to sit back, look at and savour this subtle communication of God with me. God might speak to you through a book you are reading, a friend, a conversation, a TV program, a billboard that you've walked by or driven past. He can even speak through a t-shirt. God is communicating with us every time we wake in the morning, step out under the sun or sit for conversation with another person. The universe and all created things say something to us about God, and He can speak to us through any of these.

Some people hear God speak to them through their feelings. Other people don't feel it in their feelings at all. They experience it in their thinking. They might be far more academic about how they go through it. People experience and observe God in many different ways.

At this point of my time in my personal prayer with God, I do the "O." It is a silent time. It is a time of stillness, and that's why you do not want to be distracted. It's a time of listening. This is not a time to be reading.

At the end of "O" I might write in my journal, "I feel like God is saying..." Time will tell if I have heard correctly.

Sometimes I believe God is impressing something on me, but very often there is just silence. The benefit of these times of silence comes from simply being open to God. Matter of fact, hearing from God doesn't happen all that often. Often, "O" can be just listening, and getting a sense of the presence of God, and that is it. Sometimes, I don't even get a sense of the presence of God. Sometimes all I can say is, "I put in my time with God today."

CHAPTER TWENTY-SEVEN

Nourish

The "N" stands for "Nourish." All healthy growing beings need nourishment. God inspired people to write the Bible. It is God's word to us. It feeds us and nourishes us. It causes us to mature in our spiritual life.

In most modern Bibles, the editors have put small headings above each story as you can see below. Take one of these small sections and read it. No more, just one small section. Read it three or four times. As you read, allow the Holy Spirit to bring it alive. It's not a dead book!

MATTHEW 5

Prayer in secret

5'And when you pray, do not imitate the hypocrites: they love to say their prayers standing up in the synagogues and at the street corners for people to see them. In truth I tell you, they have had their reward.6But when you pray, go to your private room, shut yourself in, and so pray to your Father who is in that secret place, and your Father who sees all that is done in secret will reward you.

How to pray - the Lord's Prayer

7In your prayers do not babble as the gentiles do, for they think that by using many words they will make themselves heard.8Do not be like them; your Father knows what you need before you ask Him.9So you should pray like this: Our Father in heaven, may your name be held holy,10your kingdom come, your will be done, on earth as in heaven.11Give us today our daily bread.12And forgive us our debts, as we have forgiven those who are in debt to us.13And do not put us to the test, but save us from the Evil One. 14Yes, if you forgive others their failings, your heavenly Father will forgive you yours;15but if you do not forgive others, your Father will not forgive your failings either.

Fasting in secret

¹⁶*When you are fasting, do not put on a gloomy look as the hypocrites do: they go about looking unsightly to let people know they are fasting. In truth I tell you, they have had their reward.*¹⁷*But when you fast, put scent on your head and wash your face,*¹⁸*so that no one will know you are fasting except your Father who sees all that is done in secret; and your Father who sees all that is done in secret will reward you.*

True treasures

¹⁹*Do not store up treasures for yourselves on earth, where moth and woodworm destroy them and thieves can break in and steal.*²⁰*But store up treasures for yourselves in heaven, where neither moth nor woodworm destroys them and thieves cannot break in and steal.*²¹*For wherever your treasure is, there will your heart be too.*

The eye, the lamp of the body

²²*The lamp of the body is the eye. It follows that if your eye is clear, your whole body will be filled with light.*²³*But if your eye is diseased, your whole body will be darkness. If then, the light inside you is darkened, what darkness that will be!*

Many of the sermons and talks that I give come from my time of "N" during my personal prayer.

The Bible is not just words about God. IT IS THE WORD OF GOD. God is present in it to us.

I am constantly amazed by its truth and relevance to my personal world.

There are parts of the Bible that are hard to understand without researching what it means. Concentrate on what you do understand, and you will be surprised how much of the other material in the Bible begins to make sense in time.

Now remember just a few verses only and do not read for your whole prayer time. Jesus asked His Father to send the Holy Spirit to help us. So ask the Holy Spirit to help you hear and understand God's words of encouragement, correction and direction for your life.

CHAPTER TWENTY-EIGHT

Ask

Now it's time for "A" for "Ask." Jesus repeatedly encouraged us to ask God for our needs. Ask! Just as a loving parent would love to give their children what they require, God wants to give us the things that we need.

Ask for God's help. If it's in your relationships, family or areas where you're trying to grow personally, in your church, for the world, for any particular need, ask God for help.

Someone said this, "Pray the largest prayers you can. You cannot think of prayers so large that God in answering it would not have wished that you had made it larger."

The Bible tells us, Glory be to Him whose power, working in us, can do infinitely more than we can ask or imagine.

Ephesians 3:20 NJB

Think of the biggest thing that you can imagine. God can top it.

I should point out that sometimes God does not want to meet the requests that we feel are so important because He has a perspective that is different to ours. God sees and understands differently to us.

For my thoughts are not your thoughts and your ways are not my ways, declares Yahweh. ⁹For the heavens are as high above earth as my ways are above your ways, my thoughts above your thoughts.

Isaiah 55:8-9 NJB

This Scripture tells us that God has the complete and perfect view while we are limited in our understanding in so many ways.

When you pray ask God for what you need or even want but trust that no matter what, He will work all things for good.

He wants us to ask — so ask for stuff.

CHAPTER TWENTY-NINE

Leave

Finally is the letter "L." I never write "L" in my journal because "L" stands for "Leave." We are not meant to stay in our daily prayer time all day, we are meant to go to our jobs, to school and university and to go out with family and friends. We are directed by God to go out and be in the world, and to take the experience of meeting God in our personal prayer out into the world.

Thank God for your time in prayer and then go and be His servant and light in the world wherever that is for you.

When I'm leaving, I say, "God, come with me today as I go throughout my day."

CHAPTER THIRTY

Keeping a Prayer Journal

I would encourage you to keep a Prayer Journal. It is a record of your relationship with God.

I have kept a Prayer Journal since I was fifteen years old, and now as I look over the last thirty odd years I can see how God has been at work in my life over that time by reading about my prayer life with God. It has built my belief and faith in God like few other things in my life. When I consider the direction of my life, what I believe God has said to me or how He has led me or what have been the deepest prayers of my life, I have a record of it in my prayer journal.

I use an ordinary spiral-bound notebook, and every time I have my personal prayer time I use it. Rosemary and other women I know have pretty coloured journals that come in all shapes and sizes. I observe that men tend to have plain notebooks. (A word from experience is if you buy the same size they stack on a bookshelf easier over time. Rosemary tells me this is not important!)

A prayer journal is not a diary or a record of the things that are happening in your life but rather a record of your spiritual relationship with God. This does not mean that I do not write down significant events like when I got married or the birth of a child, but I do not write down the circumstances of the event in long hand. If I want to do so, I do this outside my designated prayer time, otherwise I spend my whole time recording the day-to-day events of my life. This is the biggest trap with keeping a prayer journal. You can spend your whole prayer time writing, and this can be a distraction to prayer. As a matter of fact, little prayer might even take place.

When I commence my time of prayer, I ensure I have a Bible, pen and journal.

I commence by writing down the day, date and time like the following:

Tuesday 16/8/05 // 9.15am-9.30am// 15 minutes

I have found by writing down the time that I begin my prayer I am not always clock-watching during prayer. This can be very distracting.

At the conclusion of my prayer time I will write down the time I finish and then how long I prayed for. I have found that by seeing the time I prayed I remain faithful to the time commitment I made to pray.

This description of how to use a Prayer Journal needs to be read in conjunction with the previous chapters on each of the steps in the Personal Prayer model.

When using your journal, commence by writing the letter of the acronym that you are up to.

Commence by writing the letter "P" for Perspective. Sometimes I might write something down after the letter, but most often I do not. The action focuses my mind on the fact that at that point, I am in the Perspective stage of my prayer.

Then I will write "E" for Everything. Once again, I might write in my journal regarding giving my all to God.

Then I will write the two "Rs" for Real or Repentance. This is where I will often write to God about how I am in my relationship with Him and the way I am living my Christian life. This is also a time when I ask His forgiveness should there be areas I need to repent for.

VERY IMPORTANT NOTE: **Do Not** write down the specific areas of weakness or sinfulness that you are repenting of in your journal. You can do this mentally. While Prayer Journals are private property, people wrongfully, from time to time, read them. It is not necessary for other people to know your weaknesses and sin unless you choose to reveal it to them.

Then I will write "S" for Salute. Here I write my prayers of praise and worship to God.

Then I will write "O" for Observe. Here I am silent before God. Should I feel God impress words on my heart, I write them down.

Then I will write "N" for Nourish. Modern Bibles have small headings that have been added by the publishers for each small story. I will read one of these and reflect on it. Should an aspect stand out to me from the passage, I will write it down. As mentioned in the chapters on Observe and Nourish, these are both interchangeable. The Scripture may cause you to once again listen to God with your heart.

Then I will write "A" for Ask. At the back of my prayer journal, I write my requests to God. By having them at the back of the journal they are all in one place, and I pray consistently for these intentions every day.

"L" stands for leave. Here I might write a final prayer and ask God to be with me that day. Normally, however, I just say this as a prayer.

If I miss praying on a day, I will still write the day and date and then write "did not pray." Then on the current day I would in the "R" for repent ask God's forgiveness for my slackness in not praying the previous day or days if that was the reason.

Should you have a Spiritual Director or are in a faith sharing small group, taking your prayer journal along enables you to share deeply and accurately what you believe God is doing in your life and how you are travelling spiritually.

During times of reflection or when I go on retreat, I will go back and read my prayer journals. I am often amazed at how God has worked in my life. They have increased my faith because I can see before my eyes what God has done in me through the years. My journals have convinced me that God is not silent but so deeply in love with us. He desires so much to lead and guide us in our lives.

When I have gone through periods of doubt and struggle with my faith and life, as we all do, I read my prayer journals. They remind me of God's word and promises to me, and of the victories that I have experienced because of my faith in God. When I read my journals, I am encouraged and renewed by them every time.

CHAPTER THIRTY-ONE

For the Easily Distracted – Write Out Your Prayers

One of the things that I often do in my prayer journal is write out my prayers in my own handwriting. I live a busy life and am constantly being asked to make decisions about so many matters. I find that when I sit to pray I often start to think about the many issues before me.

I also get distracted very easily, and I find myself thinking about all kinds of things, not just work and ministry. I once heard of someone who said that during their personal prayer they write out their prayers. I remember when I first heard this, I thought to myself, "How weird is that?" but being so easily distracted I decided one day to give it a go. I was surprised just how focused it kept me. It takes a little getting used to and I do not do it all the time, but I always write at least the date and the letters of P.E.R.S.O.N.A.L. in my journal every day.

I would write in my prayer journal something like this. "Dear God, I love you – I worship you. I honour you. You are the one. You're the centre of my life. You are the first. Lord, don't let me stray...etc."

I'll write pages of the stuff and then read it back during my prayer. It often leads me to just sitting before God in awe and silence.

CHAPTER THIRTY-TWO

Make a Decision to Pray

If you have gotten this far, you must be keen to develop your relationship with God. Keep this book with your Bible and journal and re-read parts that might help you as you grow in your prayer life.

Here is a summary:

1. Make a decision to pray.

2. Choose a place.

3. Choose a time.

4. Decide for how long.

5. Follow the P.E.R.S.O.N.A.L. Prayer Steps

Perspective

Everything

Real and Repent

Salute

Observe

Nourish

Ask

Leave

Be glad for all God is planning for you. Be patient in trouble and be prayerful always.

Be joyful in hope, persevere in hardship; keep praying regularly
Romans 12:12 NJB

Prayer takes practice. Some days it will be fantastic, while other days it will be just like any relationship, a little flat. It is in the flat times that we have to persist. There will be days when two hours does not seem long and other days when three minutes seems like an eternity.

There is much we can learn from others about how to pray. It is how I have learnt to pray.

CHAPTER THIRTY-THREE

Prayer of Commitment

Prayer is the DEEPEST part of us yearning for something outside us. It is the depths of us seeking more. It is the deepest part of us reaching out to something that is beyond our limitations. Prayer is a search for truth; it is attempting to understand what is real. It is accepting that we are made by one more powerful than us.

Prayer is knowing that we aren't "Top of the Hill," but that there is someone higher up that we are dependent on. Prayer is our groaning, it's the honesty at our core saying, "I want more out of life." It's our self-longing to be accepted into the arms of God for who we are, knowing that we need Him for our happiness and our completion.

What is prayer? Prayer is saying, "Hello." Prayer is saying, "Here I am." Prayer is saying, "I need you. Touch me, form me, direct me, guide me, love me!" Prayer is you on your most honest day saying, "I want Your will in my life, and would You please show up and tell me what to do."

Prayer is the deepest part of us coming honestly before God.

How do you do it?

Every day be disciplined. Realise that there are days when you'll feel great and that there will be days when you feel poor. Take it to your mentors and your friends and share with them how you are going.

We learn that prayer will develop in the same way that we learn the skills to have deep conversation with a friend. In time, we will learn dependence on God.

One person's prayer will be different to another person's prayer and that's OK, because God, who is a multi-faceted God, who created all of us in His reflection and image and likeness, can understand the prayers of every one of us. Pray each day, and you will grow, and your life will be changed for eternity.

"Lord I commit to spending time with You where our relationship can grow and deepen. I will not walk away from this commitment. May we get to know each other deeply and truly. Please help me to be faithful and consistent."

AMEN

CPSIA information can be obtained
at www.ICGtesting.com
Printed in the USA
LVHW081439091118
596563LV00016B/584/P

9 781947 426009